The Old Farmer's Almanac
2009
ENGAGEMENT
CALENDAR

Begin the new year square with every man.

–Robert B. Thomas, founder of
The Old Farmer's Almanac (1766–1846)

from the editors of The Old Farmer's Almanac

Writer: Heidi Stonehill • *Calendar editor:* Martie Majoros • *Art director:* Margo Letourneau
Contributors: Janice Stillman, Mare-Anne Jarvela, Jack Burnett, Sarah Perreault, and Celeste Longacre

Astronomical events are given in U.S. Eastern Standard Time or U.S. Eastern Daylight Time.

Cover painting: Secrets of the Morning I, by Max Hayslette

About the cover artist:
Max Hayslette currently resides in Kingston, Washington. Influenced by Asian masters, he is well-known for his landscape paintings, which evoke a warm and gentle, spiritual quality. His work is included in over 300 private, corporate, and public collections and has been exhibited internationally.

This calendar belongs to:

Name _____

Address _____

Phone:

Home/Work/Cell _____ / _____ / _____

E-mail _____

The Old Farmer's Almanac, P.O. Box 520, Dublin, New Hampshire 03444
Publisher: Sherin Pierce

To order your copies of The Old Farmer's Almanac Engagement Calendar, call 800-ALMANAC or visit our Web site at **shop.Almanac.com.**

For wholesale information, contact Cindy Schlosser at 800-729-9265, ext. 126, or Stacey Korpi, ext. 160.

PRINTED IN U.S.A.

ISBN-13: 978-1-57198-459-3

2009

bold = *U.S. federal and/or Canadian national holidays*

JANUARY

S	M	T	W	T	F	S
				1	2	3
4	5	6	7	8	9	10
11	12	13	14	15	16	17
18	**19**	20	21	22	23	24
25	26	27	28	29	30	31

FEBRUARY

S	M	T	W	T	F	S
1	2	3	4	5	6	7
8	9	10	11	12	13	14
15	**16**	17	18	19	20	21
22	23	24	25	26	27	28

MARCH

S	M	T	W	T	F	S
1	2	3	4	5	6	7
8	9	10	11	12	13	14
15	16	17	18	19	20	21
22	23	24	25	26	27	28
29	30	31				

APRIL

S	M	T	W	T	F	S
			1	2	3	4
5	6	7	8	9	**10**	11
12	**13**	14	15	16	17	18
19	20	21	22	23	24	25
26	27	28	29	30		

MAY

S	M	T	W	T	F	S
					1	2
3	4	5	6	7	8	9
10	11	12	13	14	15	16
17	**18**	19	20	21	22	23
24	**25**	26	27	28	29	30
31						

JUNE

S	M	T	W	T	F	S
	1	2	3	4	5	6
7	8	9	10	11	12	13
14	15	16	17	18	19	20
21	22	23	24	25	26	27
28	29	30				

JULY

S	M	T	W	T	F	S
			1	2	3	**4**
5	6	7	8	9	10	11
12	13	14	15	16	17	18
19	20	21	22	23	24	25
26	27	28	29	30	31	

AUGUST

S	M	T	W	T	F	S
						1
2	3	4	5	6	7	8
9	10	11	12	13	14	15
16	17	18	19	20	21	22
23	24	25	26	27	28	29
30	31					

SEPTEMBER

S	M	T	W	T	F	S
		1	2	3	4	5
6	**7**	8	9	10	11	12
13	14	15	16	17	18	19
20	21	22	23	24	25	26
27	28	29	30			

OCTOBER

S	M	T	W	T	F	S
				1	2	3
4	5	6	7	8	9	10
11	**12**	13	14	15	16	17
18	19	20	21	22	23	24
25	26	27	28	29	30	31

NOVEMBER

S	M	T	W	T	F	S
1	2	3	4	5	6	7
8	9	10	**11**	12	13	14
15	16	17	18	19	20	21
22	23	24	25	**26**	27	28
29	30					

DECEMBER

S	M	T	W	T	F	S
		1	2	3	4	5
6	7	8	9	10	11	12
13	14	15	16	17	18	19
20	21	22	23	24	**25**	**26**
27	28	29	30	31		

MONTHLY REMINDERS

Which president held the first New Year's Day reception at the White House?

John Adams, in 1801.

What's Your Sign?

CAPRICORN

DECEMBER 22–JANUARY 19

Symbol: ♑ *The Mountain Goat*
Ruling Planet: *Saturn*
Element: *Earth*
Quality: *Discipline*
Ability: *Working for goals*
Traits: *Capable, efficient, ambitious, witty*

Full Wolf Moon

To Your Health

What should you do if you sprain your ankle? Call your doctor and remember P-R-I-C-E:

Protection—Use a splint, brace, or bandage wrap to support your ankle and help to restrict movement.

Rest—Rest your ankle; avoid activities that cause pain. Use crutches if it is painful to walk. Do this especially for the first 2 days. After this time, it is best to begin to use the ankle gently.

Ice—As soon as possible, cover the injured area with a cloth, then apply an ice pack for 15 to 20 minutes every 2 to 3 hours while awake. Do this for the first 3 days. This will reduce pain, swelling, and inflammation.

Compression—Wrap an elastic wrap or bandage from toes to midcalf, using even pressure. Wear until the swelling goes down. Loosen if circulation is hampered. This will help to prevent extra fluid from settling around the injured area.

Elevate—Raise the ankle above heart level to minimize swelling. Try to do this at least 2 to 3 hours during each day and at night while sleeping.

This month's full Moon got its name from the hungry wolves that were on the prowl now. It is also known as the Old Moon.

❧

When oak trees bend with snow in January, good crops may be expected.

AGE-OLD ADVICE

For a sprain, bathe in good crab verjuice [an acidic juice made from pressed, unripe crab apples].

–Consult Me, *1902*

𝓛et us start off right and pay up the little bills first, for it is a well-known maxim that well begun is half done.

–The Old Farmer's Almanac, *January 1884*

DECEMBER 2008 ❧ JANUARY 2009

29 *Monday*

Islamic New Year

*There is no pillow
so soft as a clear
conscience.*

–French proverb

30 *Tuesday*

Before putting away
Christmas tree lights,
replace any that are
not working.

31 *Wednesday*

*There is always
something to learn that
will aid us to do better
and more intelligent
work next year.*

–The Old Farmer's Almanac, *1887*

1 *Thursday*

New Year's Day

Eating black-eyed
peas today brings
good luck.

JANUARY • 2009

S	M	T	W	T	F	S
				1	2	3
4	5	6	7	8	9	10
11	12	13	14	15	16	17
18	19	20	21	22	23	24
25	26	27	28	29	30	31

FEBRUARY • 2009

S	M	T	W	T	F	S
1	2	3	4	5	6	7
8	9	10	11	12	13	14
15	16	17	18	19	20	21
22	23	24	25	26	27	28

Friday

2

No book is of much importance; the vital thing is, What do you yourself think?

–Elbert Hubbard, American writer (1856–1915)

Saturday

3

Look for the Quadrantid meteor showers before dawn tomorrow.

Sunday

4

First Quarter

On this day in 1643, physicist Sir Isaac Newton was born.

REMINDERS

....
....
....
....
....
....

JANUARY

5 Monday

**Sneezes, then freezes
noses and kneeses.**
–The Old Farmer's Almanac, *1966*

6 Tuesday

Epiphany

On this day, it is a
Mexican tradition to
serve *Rosca de Reyes,* a
sweet bread with a
figure of baby Jesus
hidden inside.

7 Wednesday

Sponge off your
houseplants or give
them a good shower
with tepid water to
remove the dust.

8 Thursday

A thermometer in
Baker, California, is
134 feet high—one of
the world's tallest.

JANUARY • 2009

S	M	T	W	T	F	S
				1	2	3
4	5	6	7	8	9	10
11	12	13	14	15	16	17
18	19	20	21	22	23	24
25	26	27	28	29	30	31

FEBRUARY • 2009

S	M	T	W	T	F	S
1	2	3	4	5	6	7
8	9	10	11	12	13	14
15	16	17	18	19	20	21
22	23	24	25	26	27	28

Friday **9**

To relieve rheumatism, wear red garters.

Saturday **10**

Full Wolf Moon

Even if a farmer intends to loaf, he gets up in time to get an early start.

–Edgar Watson Howe, American writer (1853–1937)

Sunday **11**

Gladiolus comes from a Latin word meaning "little sword," due to the shape of the leaves.

REMINDERS

....
....
....
....
....

JANUARY

12 *Monday*

Today is a good day
to entertain.

13 *Tuesday*

Drink rosemary
tea to enhance your
memory.

14 *Wednesday*

*Skating teaches you
to do the things you
should do before you
do the things you
want to do.*

–Barbara Ann Scott, Canadian
figure skater (b. 1928)

15 *Thursday*

On this day in 1919,
the Great Molasses
Flood damaged areas
of Boston.

JANUARY • 2009

S M T W T F S
1 2 3
4 5 6 7 8 9 10
11 12 13 14 15 16 17
18 19 20 21 22 23 24
25 26 27 28 29 30 31

FEBRUARY • 2009

S M T W T F S
1 2 3 4 5 6 7
8 9 10 11 12 13 14
15 16 17 18 19 20 21
22 23 24 25 26 27 28

Friday 16

To deter cats from
digging into the soil
of large houseplants,
place decorative
rocks on top.

Saturday 17

Benjamin Franklin's
Birthday
Last Quarter

*The discontented man
finds no easy chair.*

–Benjamin Franklin, American
statesman (1706–90)

Sunday 18

After scrambling
eggs, add salted water
to the frying pan for
easy cleanup later.

REMINDERS

....

....

....

....

....

....

JANUARY

19 *Monday*

Martin Luther King Jr.'s
Birthday (observed)

*. . . even though we
face the difficulties of
today and tomorrow, I
still have a dream.*

*–Martin Luther King Jr.,
American civil rights leader
(1929–68)*

20 *Tuesday*

The borders of
Colorado, New
Mexico, Arizona, and
Utah meet at one
point—the only
four-state junction
in the nation.

21 *Wednesday*

A warm January,
a cold May.

22 *Thursday*

Use natural-bristle
brushes with oil-based
paint and synthetic
brushes with latex.

JANUARY • 2009

S	M	T	W	T	F	S
				1	2	3
4	5	6	7	8	9	10
11	12	13	14	15	16	17
18	19	20	21	22	23	24
25	26	27	28	29	30	31

FEBRUARY • 2009

S	M	T	W	T	F	S
1	2	3	4	5	6	7
8	9	10	11	12	13	14
15	16	17	18	19	20	21
22	23	24	25	26	27	28

Friday **23**

If your feet start to itch for no apparent reason, you'll soon start a journey to a new place.

Saturday **24**

*When I was born,
I was so surprised I
didn't talk for a year
and a half.*

*—Gracie Allen, American
comedienne (1902–64)*

Sunday **25**

Today is a good day to
end old projects.

Complement this calendar with daily weather and Almanac wit and wisdom at Almanac.com.

26 *Monday*

Chinese New Year
New Moon

Today starts
the Chinese year of
the ox.

27 *Tuesday*

*It is better to deserve
without receiving,
than to receive without
deserving.*

–Robert Green Ingersoll, American
lawyer (1833–99)

28 *Wednesday*

**Married in blue,
he will always be true.**

29 *Thursday*

On this day in 1900,
the American Baseball
League was founded
in Chicago.

JANUARY • 2009   FEBRUARY • 2009

S M T W T F S   S M T W T F S
            1 2 3   1 2 3 4 5 6 7
4 5 6 7 8 9 10   8 9 10 11 12 13 14
11 12 13 14 15 16 17   15 16 17 18 19 20 21
18 19 20 21 22 23 24   22 23 24 25 26 27 28
25 26 27 28 29 30 31

*Luck is like having
a rice dumpling fly into
your mouth.*

—*Japanese proverb*

Friday **30**

To remove soot from
woodstove glass, use a
damp newspaper
dipped in cold ashes.

Saturday **31**

On a diet?
Add fennel leaves to
salads to curb your
appetite.

Sunday **1**

REMINDERS

....

....

....

....

....

....

FEBRUARY with *The Old Farmer's Almanac*

MONTHLY REMINDERS

ASK THE ALMANAC

*How can you remove ballpoint ink stains
from washable fabric?*

Place the fabric ink-side down on white paper
towels. Gently dab the stain with rubbing
alcohol. Blot with a clean, white cloth until
the stain disappears. Rinse thoroughly with
the hottest water that is safe for the fabric.

What's Your Sign?

AQUARIUS

JANUARY 20–FEBRUARY 19

Symbol: ≈ *The Water Bearer*
Ruling planet: *Uranus*
Element: *Air*
Quality: *Inventiveness*
Ability: *To see the future*
Traits: *Enthusiastic, tolerant, independent*

Full Snow Moon

To Your Health

According to USDA dietary guidelines, a daily diet should include the following (based on 2,000 calories per day*):

GRAINS

6 daily servings, of which at least three should be whole-wheat. One serving equals a 1-ounce slice of bread, 1 cup of dry cereal, or ½ cup of cooked cereal, rice, or pasta.

VEGETABLES

2 ½ cups. Include vegetables of all colors to get a variety of nutrients and minerals.

FRUITS

2 cups. Include fruits of all colors to get a variety of nutrients and minerals.

FATS

6 teaspoons. Fish, vegetable oils, and nuts should be the primary sources.

MILK AND DAIRY

3 cups (low-fat or no-fat).

MEAT AND BEANS

5 ½ ounces. Select lean meats, such as skinless poultry, beef sirloin, or pork tenderloin. Substitute cooked dry beans, fish, eggs, nuts, and seeds for meats three times per week.

*To modify this diet based on age, gender, and physical activity, visit www.mypyramid.gov.

AGE-OLD ADVICE

The manufacture of sugar is comparatively a late matter. A hundred years or so ago, people got along without it except as naturally present in their foods.

–Alice Peloubet Norton, Food and Dietetics, 1904

This month's full Moon got its name because the heaviest snows of the year usually fall now. Hunting at this time of year became difficult for many Native American tribes, so they also called this the Hunger Moon.

When gnats dance in February, the husbandman becomes a beggar.

A warm bed is a cozy thing these cold nights.
–The Old Farmer's Almanac, February 1884

February

2 *Monday*

Candlemas
Groundhog Day
First Quarter

It's not fit out for men or marmots.

–The Old Farmer's Almanac, *1997*

3 *Tuesday*

Today is a good day to cut hair to encourage growth.

4 *Wednesday*

Many stars in winter indicate frost.

5 *Thursday*

Keep all combustibles at least 3 feet away from woodstoves, heaters, and furnaces.

FEBRUARY • 2009

S M T W T F S
1 2 3 4 5 6 7
8 9 10 11 12 13 14
15 16 17 18 19 20 21
22 23 24 25 26 27 28

MARCH • 2009

S M T W T F S
1 2 3 4 5 6 7
8 9 10 11 12 13 14
15 16 17 18 19 20 21
22 23 24 25 26 27 28
29 30 31

*The discovery of a
new dish does more for
the happiness of
mankind than the
discovery of a new star.*

*–Anthelme Brillat-Savarin,
French writer (1755–1826)*

Friday

6

A group of kittens is
called a kindle.

Saturday

7

In colonial times,
wallpaper was hung
with tacks, not paste.

Sunday

8

REMINDERS

....
....
....
....
....
....

February

9 *Monday*

Full Snow Moon

Icicles tend to form more often on the south sides of buildings.

10 *Tuesday*

To see oysters in your dream is a sign of prosperity.

11 *Wednesday*

To add humidity for houseplants, set pots on trays of pebbles. Fill the trays with water to just below the bottom of the pots.

12 *Thursday*

Abraham Lincoln's Birthday

His love shone as impartial as the Sun.

–from "Lincoln's Grave" by James Maurice Thompson, American writer (1844–1901)

FEBRUARY • 2009

S M T W T F S
1 2 3 4 5 6 7
8 9 10 11 12 13 14
15 16 17 18 19 20 21
22 23 24 25 26 27 28

MARCH • 2009

S M T W T F S
1 2 3 4 5 6 7
8 9 10 11 12 13 14
15 16 17 18 19 20 21
22 23 24 25 26 27 28
29 30 31

Friday 13

This year has three
Fridays the 13th—
in February, March,
and November.

Saturday 14

Valentine's Day

In order to recognize
each other, prairie dogs
"kiss" by touching
teeth.

Sunday 15

Susan B. Anthony's
Birthday (Fla., Wis.)
National Flag of Canada Day

The world's largest
carousel, in Spring
Green, Wisconsin, is
80 feet in diameter
and has 269 animals.

REMINDERS

....
....
....
....
....
....

FEBRUARY

16 Monday

George Washington's
Birthday (observed)
Family Day (Alta.,
Ont., Sask., Can.)
Last Quarter

Extremes meet.

17 Tuesday

*Truth is immortal;
error is mortal.*

–Mary Baker Eddy, American
humanitarian (1821–1910)

18 Wednesday

Tulipa probably
came from a Turkish
word for "turban,"
a reference to the
flower's shape.

19 Thursday

A light-year is the
distance that light
can travel in a vacuum
(such as space)
in a year—about
6 trillion miles.

FEBRUARY • 2009

S	M	T	W	T	F	S
1	2	3	4	5	6	7
8	9	10	11	12	13	14
15	16	17	18	19	20	21
22	23	24	25	26	27	28

MARCH • 2009

S	M	T	W	T	F	S
1	2	3	4	5	6	7
8	9	10	11	12	13	14
15	16	17	18	19	20	21
22	23	24	25	26	27	28
29	30	31				

Heritage Day (Y.T., Can.)

Friday **20**

*Q: On what kind of
ships do students study?*
A: Scholarships.

To avoid catching a cold, wear a necklace of blue beads.

Saturday **21**

---

*First in war,
first in peace, and first
in the hearts of his
countrymen.*

Sunday **22**

*–said of George Washington by
Henry Lee, American politician
(1756–1818)*

REMINDERS

....

....

....

....

....

....

23 *Monday*

To prevent migraines, drink feverfew tea.

24 *Tuesday*

Mardi Gras (Ala.; La.)
New Moon

Thunder on Shrove Tuesday [today] foretelleth wind, store of fruit, and plenty.

25 *Wednesday*

Ash Wednesday

On this day in 1841, painter Pierre-Auguste Renoir was born.

26 *Thursday*

To freshen smelly sneakers, sprinkle the insides with salt, wait 24 hours, and then shake the salt out.

FEBRUARY • 2009   MARCH • 2009

S M T W T F S   S M T W T F S
1 2 3 4 5 6 7   1 2 3 4 5 6 7
8 9 10 11 12 13 14   8 9 10 11 12 13 14
15 16 17 18 19 20 21   15 16 17 18 19 20 21
22 23 24 25 26 27 28   22 23 24 25 26 27 28
                   29 30 31

It is the humble work
that makes life noble.
–The Old Farmer's Almanac, *1873*

Friday 27

Monopoly is the
most-played board
game in the world.

Saturday 28

"March comes in like a
lion" may have referred
to the constellation Leo
rising higher in the east.

Sunday 1

REMINDERS

....
....
....
....
....
....

MARCH with *The Old Farmer's Almanac*

What does the term "once removed" mean in family relationships?

It means that the two people differ by one generation. For example, a first cousin once removed from you can be the child of a great aunt or great uncle or the child of a first cousin.

What's Your Sign?

PISCES

FEBRUARY 20–MARCH 20

Symbol: ♓ *The Fish*
Ruling planet: *Neptune*
Element: *Water*
Quality: *Creativity*
Ability: *Understanding*
Traits: *Romantic, compassionate, imaginative, introspective*

To Your Health

To keep your mouth fresh and healthy, follow these guidelines:

🦷 Brush for 2 to 3 minutes two to three times per day. Hold a soft-bristled toothbrush at a 45-degree angle to the gums and gently use circular motions and short back-and-forth strokes. Also brush your tongue. Change your toothbrush at least once every 3 months or sooner if bristles become worn or you have used it when you had a cold.

🦷 Use a fluoride toothpaste. Also use a fluoride mouth rinse (not recommended for children under 6).

🦷 Floss at least once per day. Ask your dentist to show you how to floss properly.

🦷 See your dentist at least twice per year for checkups and cleanings or as soon as possible if any problems arise.

🦷 Avoid tobacco and use alcohol only in moderation. Eat a balanced diet. Cut down on sugary, starchy snacks between meals; these promote tooth decay. Instead, try nuts, raw vegetables, apples, plain yogurt, aged cheese, or sugarless gum containing xylitol. These can actually help fight the effects of the acid produced by bacteria in the mouth. .

AGE-OLD ADVICE

Honey mixed with pure pulverized charcoal is said to be excellent to cleanse the teeth and make them white.

–Lydia Maria Child, American Frugal Housewife, *1832*

Full Worm Moon

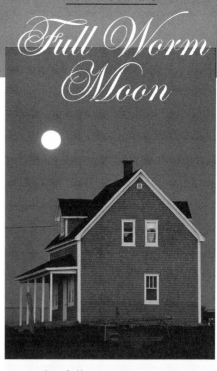

This full Moon got its name because now the ground begins to soften and earthworm casts reappear. It is also known as the Full Sap Moon because it marks the time when the maple sap begins to flow and the annual tapping of maple trees begins.

🦷

*March sun
Lets snow stand on a stone.*

We shall need to brush up the tools and get ready to use them by and by, and so you might as well take the rough days of the first part of this bleak month to do it in.

–The Old Farmer's Almanac, *March 1884*

MARCH

2 Monday

Texas Independence Day

Pintos and other dried beans are a great source of fiber.

3 Tuesday

Town Meeting Day (Vt.)

Montpelier, Vermont, has the smallest population of any state capital in the United States.

4 Wednesday

First Quarter

To remove mildew from marble, clean with diluted ammonia (½ cup ammonia per gallon of water).

5 Thursday

It is lucky for a strange dog to follow you home.

MARCH • 2009

S	M	T	W	T	F	S
1	2	3	4	5	6	7
8	9	10	11	12	13	14
15	16	17	18	19	20	21
22	23	24	25	26	27	28
29	30	31				

APRIL • 2009

S	M	T	W	T	F	S
				1	2	3	4
5	6	7	8	9	10	11
12	13	14	15	16	17	18
19	20	21	22	23	24	25
26	27	28	29	30		

Friday

6

*A successful lawsuit
is the one worn by
a policeman.*

–Robert Frost, American poet
(1874–1963)

Saturday

7

Today is a good day
to entertain.

Sunday

8

Sunday of Orthodoxy
Daylight Saving Time
begins at 2:00 A.M.

The word "fortnight"
comes from Old
English words that
mean "fourteen
nights," or two weeks.

REMINDERS

MARCH

9 | Monday

Commonwealth Day (Canada)

To have fresh mushrooms on hand for cooking, buy a mushroom kit.

10 | Tuesday

Full Worm Moon

The Night walked down the sky With the Moon in her hand.

–Frederick Lawrence Knowles American poet (1869–1905)

11 | Wednesday

A dash of salt makes cream and egg whites whip more rapidly.

12 | Thursday

Today is a good day to prune to discourage growth.

MARCH • 2009

S	M	T	W	T	F	S
1	2	3	4	5	6	7
8	9	10	11	12	13	14
15	16	17	18	19	20	21
22	23	24	25	26	27	28
29	30	31				

APRIL • 2009

S	M	T	W	T	F	S
			1	2	3	4
5	6	7	8	9	10	11
12	13	14	15	16	17	18
19	20	21	22	23	24	25
26	27	28	29	30		

Friday 13

When a school succeeds in proving to a child that all its efforts are in his behalf, half the battle is won.

–Mary Kimball Morgan, American teacher (1861–1948)

Saturday 14

On the Beaufort wind force scale, a wind speed of 19 to 24 miles per hour is called a fresh breeze.

Sunday 15

Andrew Jackson Day (Tenn.)

An old U.S. $20 bill shows the magnolia tree that Andrew Jackson planted in memory of his deceased wife.

REMINDERS

....

....

....

....

....

MARCH

16 *Monday*

The 134-mile-wide Galle Crater on Mars has ridges that form a smiling face, earning it the nickname of "Happy Face" Crater.

17 *Tuesday*

St. Patrick's Day
Evacuation Day (Suffolk Co., Mass.)

Never put your hand out farther than you can draw it back again.
—Irish proverb

18 *Wednesday*

Last Quarter

When sheep turn their backs to the wind, it is a sign of rain.

19 *Thursday*

Alyssum comes from Greek words meanin "not madness," because the plant wa once thought to cur madness and rabies

MARCH • 2009

S	M	T	W	T	F	S
1	2	3	4	5	6	7
8	9	10	11	12	13	14
15	16	17	18	19	20	21
22	23	24	25	26	27	28
29	30	31				

APRIL • 2009

S	M	T	W	T	F	S
			1	2	3	4
5	6	7	8	9	10	11
12	13	14	15	16	17	18
19	20	21	22	23	24	25
26	27	28	29	30		

Vernal Equinox

Friday **20**

*Spring in the world!
And all things are
made new!*

–Richard Hovey, American poet
(1864–1900)

No two people have
the same fingerprints
—or tongue prints.

Saturday **21**

Finding the first
spring flower on a Sunday
brings good luck.

Sunday **22**

REMINDERS

MARCH

23 *Monday*

No living man
All things can.
–English proverb

24 *Tuesday*

On this day in 1874,
magician Harry
Houdini was born.

25 *Wednesday*

*Ennui is the trouble
of those who have no
other troubles.*
–The Old Farmer's Almanac, 1901

26 *Thursday*

New Moon

Today is a good day to
start a new project.

MARCH • 2009

S M T W T F S
1 2 3 4 5 6 7
8 9 10 11 12 13 14
15 16 17 18 19 20 21
22 23 24 25 26 27 28
29 30 31

APRIL • 2009

S M T W T F S
1 2 3 4
5 6 7 8 9 10 11
12 13 14 15 16 17 18
19 20 21 22 23 24 25
26 27 28 29 30

So many frosts in March, so many in May.

Friday 27

Painting walls burns about the same amount of calories as walking normally.

Saturday 28

*The first thunder of the year awakes
All the frogs and all the snakes.*

Sunday 29

REMINDERS

....
....
....
....
....
....

30 Monday

Seward's Day (Alaska)

Politician William Seward, instrumental in the purchase of Alaska, also sheltered fugitive slaves in the Underground Railroad.

31 Tuesday

[March goes] out like a damp lamb.

–The Old Farmer's Almanac, *1979*

1 Wednesday

All Fools' Day

If your nose itches, you may kiss a fool in the near future.

2 Thursday

Pascua Florida Day
First Quarter

First and last "quarter Moons actually look like half Moons in the sky.

MARCH • 2009

S	M	T	W	T	F	S
1	2	3	4	5	6	7
8	9	10	11	12	13	14
15	16	17	18	19	20	21
22	23	24	25	26	27	28
29	30	31				

APRIL • 2009

S	M	T	W	T	F	S
			1	2	3	4
5	6	7	8	9	10	11
12	13	14	15	16	17	18
19	20	21	22	23	24	25
26	27	28	29	30		

Friday

3

For better germination, soak okra seeds overnight in a bowl of water.

Saturday

4

Today is a good day to prune to encourage growth.

Palm Sunday

Sunday

5

Leaves of date palms are often used in Christian services on this day. In the United States, most are grown in southern California.

REMINDERS

MONTHLY REMINDERS

ASK THE ALMANAC

What is the formula for estimating how many miles away an approaching thunderstorm might be?

A:

Count the seconds between a flash of lightning and the thunder that accompanies it and divide by five.

What's Your Sign?

ARIES
MARCH 21–APRIL 20

Symbol: ♈ *The Ram*
Ruling planet: *Mars*
Element: *Fire*
Quality: *Assertiveness*
Ability: *Leadership*
Traits: *Fearless, optimistic, energetic, impulsive*

To Your Health

If you experience seasonal allergies to pollen, these food compounds may help to alleviate your symptoms:

❧ **Probiotics** (beneficial bacteria), found in dietary supplements or in yogurt containing live cultures

❧ **Omega-3 fatty acids,** found in salmon, halibut, tuna, cod, sardines, fish oil, flaxseed oil, canola oil, shrimp, clams, spinach, and walnuts

❧ **Quercetin,** found in citrus, apples, cranberries, grapes, olive oil, blueberries, blackberries, onions, parsley, spinach, broccoli, kale, black and green teas, and red wine. You can also buy quercetin supplements. Research has found that quercetin is more effective when combined with bromelain, an enzyme in pineapple.

❧ **Vitamin C,** found in citrus, papaya, cantaloupe, kiwi, strawberries, parsley, bell peppers, broccoli, mustard greens, brussels sprouts, kale, cauliflower, and sweet potatoes

CAUTION: *Some people allergic to pollen may also be allergic to certain fresh fruits, vegetables, nuts, and grains.*

AGE-OLD ADVICE

Asthmas require dishes prepared from the lungs of pigs, deer, calves, hares, and lambs.

–18th-century remedy, The Old Farmer's Almanac, *1963*

Full Pink Moon

This month's full Moon got its name because wild ground phlox, one of the earliest widespread flowers of the spring, are usually in bloom around this time. It is also often called the Sprouting Grass Moon.

❧

*If it thunders on All Fools' Day
It brings good crops of corn and hay.*

If there were to be no rain till every man wanted it, the ground would go dry.

–The Old Farmer's Almanac, April 1884

April

6 *Monday*

Adopting a pet? Adult animals are usually calmer, more predictable, and less demanding.

7 *Tuesday*

To prevent a toothache, never wash on a Tuesday.

8 *Wednesday*

Moist April, clear June.

9 *Thursday*

First day of Passover
Full Pink Moon

To avoid tears, put onions in the freezer for a few minutes before slicing.

APRIL • 2009   MAY • 2009

S	M	T	W	T	F	S
			1	2	3	4
5	6	7	8	9	10	11
12	13	14	15	16	17	18
19	20	21	22	23	24	25
26	27	28	29	30		

S	M	T	W	T	F	S
					1	2
3	4	5	6	7	8	9
10	11	12	13	14	15	16
17	18	19	20	21	22	23
24	25	26	27	28	29	30
31						

Good Friday — Friday 10

Phlox comes from a Greek word for "flame," because the flowers are brightly colored.

Saturday 11

Keep clover in your lawn—it adds nitrogen to the soil.

Easter — Sunday 12

A chicken's eggshell has between 6,000 and 8,000 pores, which allow the exchange of oxygen and carbon dioxide.

REMINDERS

APRIL

13 *Monday*

Easter Monday
Thomas Jefferson's
Birthday

Thomas Jefferson
invented the swivel
chair.

14 *Tuesday*

Listen for the
dandelion's roar.

–The Old Farmer's Almanac, *1985*

15 *Wednesday*

Under ideal
conditions, 336
trillion houseflies
could develop from
a single pair in one
season—if they all
survive.

16 *Thursday*

A tennis racket with
a large head gives you
more power but
less control than a
smaller one.

APRIL • 2009

S	M	T	W	T	F	S
			1	2	3	4
5	6	7	8	9	10	11
12	13	14	15	16	17	18
19	20	21	22	23	24	25
26	27	28	29	30		

MAY • 2009

S	M	T	W	T	F	S
					1	2
3	4	5	6	7	8	9
10	11	12	13	14	15	16
17	18	19	20	21	22	23
24	25	26	27	28	29	30
31						

Last Quarter

A sweating stone indicates rain soon.

Friday 17

Place a snail in a pan of cornmeal. The snail's tracks will spell your true love's initials.

Saturday 18

Orthodox Easter

Today is a good day to begin a diet to lose weight.

Sunday 19

REMINDERS

Complement this calendar with daily weather and Almanac wit and wisdom at Almanac.com.

April

20 Monday

Patriots Day (Maine, Mass.)

Revere Beach, established in 1896 in Revere, Massachusetts, was the first public beach in the United States.

21 Tuesday

San Jacinto Day (Tex.)

If your ears ring at night, it could mean that the wind will change.

22 Wednesday

Earth Day

I am a passenger on the spaceship Earth.

–R. Buckminster Fuller, American engineer (1895–1983)

23 Thursday

St. George's Day (N.L., Can.)

To remove rust from tinware, rub it with a peeled potato dipped in baking soda.

APRIL • 2009

S	M	T	W	T	F	S
			1	2	3	4
5	6	7	8	9	10	11
12	13	14	15	16	17	18
19	20	21	22	23	24	25
26	27	28	29	30		

MAY • 2009

S	M	T	W	T	F	S
					1	2
3	4	5	6	7	8	9
10	11	12	13	14	15	16
17	18	19	20	21	22	23
24	25	26	27	28	29	30
31						

National Arbor Day
New Moon

Friday **24**

Birthday of Robert B.
Thomas (1766–1846),
founder of *The Old
Farmer's Almanac.*

Too much fertilizer
will discourage
lilac bushes from
flowering.

Saturday **25**

Oranges, apples, and
carrots contain pectin,
which helps to reduce
cholesterol and curb
your appetite.

Sunday **26**

REMINDERS

....
....
....
....
....
....

27 Monday

The sun, the open air, silence, and art are great physicians.
–Santiago Ramon y Cajal, Spanish neuroscientist (1852–1934)

28 Tuesday

Q: What happens when it rains cats and dogs?
A: You have to be careful not to step in a poodle.

29 Wednesday

Everyone has a gift for something, even if it is the gift of being a good friend.
–Marian Anderson, American singer (1897–1993)

30 Thursday

The first U.S. presidential inauguration occurred on this day in 1789.

APRIL • 2009

S M T W T F S
         1 2 3 4
5 6 7 8 9 10 11
12 13 14 15 16 17 18
19 20 21 22 23 24 25
26 27 28 29 30

MAY • 2009

S M T W T F S
            1 2
3 4 5 6 7 8 9
10 11 12 13 14 15 16
17 18 19 20 21 22 23
24 25 26 27 28 29 30
31

May Day
First Quarter

Friday

1

Today is a good day
to entertain.

Bread will stay
fresher longer if you
put a piece of celery
in the bag.

Saturday

2

In honor of National
Pet Week, make sure
that your pet is up-to-
date on its vaccinations.

Sunday

3

REMINDERS

....

....

....

....

....

MAY with *The Old Farmer's Almanac*

ASK THE ALMANAC

What is the difference between determinate and indeterminate tomatoes?

Determinate tomatoes stop growing after a certain point and set flower and fruit in a short period of time. Indeterminate tomatoes continue to grow and set flower and fruit until frost.

What's Your Sign?

TAURUS
APRIL 21–MAY 20

Symbol: ♉ *The Bull*
Ruling planet: *Venus*
Element: *Earth*
Quality: *Practical*
Ability: *Persistence*
Traits: *Determined, domestic, thorough, nurturing*

Full Flower Moon

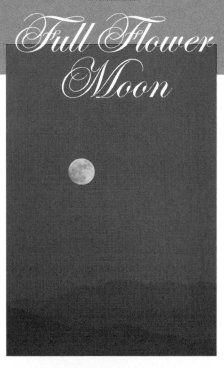

This month's full Moon got its name because flowers spring forth in abundance at this time. Some Algonquin tribes knew this Moon as the Corn Planting Moon or the Milk Moon.

🦋

*He who mows in May
Will have neither fruit nor hay.*

ear in mind the good old adage: "Act well your part; there all the honor lies."

–The Old Farmer's Almanac, *May 1884*

To Your Health

Use ergonomic tools to avoid discomfort when gardening. In hand tools, look for . . .

🦋 the correct handle size. The circumference of the handle should be the same as the circle made with your thumb and index finger.

🦋 a soft, nonslip handle that will keep your hand from cramping and be easier on the joints.

🦋 a handle contoured to fit your palm. Avoid handles with depressions for each finger, as they probably don't fit the size of your hand.

🦋 a depression in the handle for your thumb to keep your hand in the correct alignment. This will help you to avoid straining your hand, arm, and shoulder.

🦋 elongated handles to avoid bending or overreaching. This will reduce strain on your back, knees, and hips.

🦋 a comfortable weight. The tool should be durable but light enough that you don't get tired when using it.

AGE-OLD ADVICE

Remember to bend only at the hips; do not bend at the waist; this will give you a good poise and keep your back straight.

–Dr. Emma E. Walker, Beauty and Health, *1904*

MAY

4 *Monday*

To save energy,
dry laundry outdoors
on a clothesline.

5 *Tuesday*

Cinco de Mayo

Toads eat cutworms
and other garden
pests. Encourage ther
with a shallow dish o
water in the shade.

6 *Wednesday*

*Politeness is one half
good nature and the
other half good lying.*
—Mary Wilson Little, America
writer (fl. c. 190

7 *Thursday*

A dream of hay symbolize
an accumulation of
earthly goods.

MAY • 2009

S	M	T	W	T	F	S
					1	2
3	4	5	6	7	8	9
10	11	12	13	14	15	16
17	18	19	20	21	22	23
24	25	26	27	28	29	30
31						

JUNE • 2009

S	M	T	W	T	F	S
	1	2	3	4	5	6
7	8	9	10	11	12	13
14	15	16	17	18	19	20
21	22	23	24	25	26	27
28	29	30				

Truman Day (Mo.)

Friday

8

Kansas City, Missouri,
has the most fountains
(more than 200!)
of any city in the
world except for
Rome, Italy.

Full Flower Moon

Saturday

9

A spring tide occurs
today (during the full
and new Moons of
any month).

Mother's Day

Sunday

10

*The sweetest sounds to
mortals given
Are heard in Mother,
Home, and Heaven.*

–William Goldsmith Brown,
American writer (1812–1906)

REMINDERS

....
....
....
....
....
....

Complement this calendar with daily weather and Almanac wit and wisdom at Almanac.com.

May

11 *Monday*

To deter grasshoppers, place row covers over the plants from seedling through harvest.

12 *Tuesday*

It is good luck for a bride to wear green on the night before her wedding.

13 *Wednesday*

The heaviest rains fall on the leakiest house.
—*Japanese proverb*

14 *Thursday*

On this day in 1686, physicist Gabriel Daniel Fahrenheit was born.

MAY • 2009

S	M	T	W	T	F	S
					1	2
3	4	5	6	7	8	9
10	11	12	13	14	15	16
17	18	19	20	21	22	23
24	25	26	27	28	29	30
31						

JUNE • 2009

S	M	T	W	T	F	S
	1	2	3	4	5	6
7	8	9	10	11	12	13
14	15	16	17	18	19	20
21	22	23	24	25	26	27
28	29	30				

Friday 15

We blink about 11,500 times per day—that's 4.2 million times every year.

Armed Forces Day

Saturday 16

Nobody will believe in you unless you believe in yourself.

—Liberace, American pianist
(1919–87)

Last Quarter

Sunday 17

If you sneeze at the table, you'll find a new friend before the next meal.

REMINDERS

MAY

18 *Monday*

Victoria Day (Canada)

Before Victoria
became queen,
she never had her
own room.

19 *Tuesday*

Today is a
good day to plant
belowground crops.

20 *Wednesday*

*Astronomers, like
burglars and jazz
musicians, operate
best at night.*

*–Miles Kington, English
journalist (b. 1941)*

21 *Thursday*

Begonia is named after
Michel Bégon
(1638–1710), French
statesman and botany
enthusiast.

MAY • 2009

S	M	T	W	T	F	S
					1	2
3	4	5	6	7	8	9
10	11	12	13	14	15	16
17	18	19	20	21	22	23
24	25	26	27	28	29	30
31						

JUNE • 2009

S	M	T	W	T	F	S
	1	2	3	4	5	6
7	8	9	10	11	12	13
14	15	16	17	18	19	20
21	22	23	24	25	26	27
28	29	30				

National Maritime Day

Friday **22**

To easily measure
the length of the fish
that you catch, paint
dots one inch apart on
your fishing rod.

*It is very hard to
shave an egg.*

–George Herbert, English poet
(1593–1633)

Saturday **23**

New Moon

Sunday **24**

Weather lore says to
expect rain if the new Moon
falls on a Sunday.

R EMINDERS

MAY

25 *Monday*

Memorial Day (observed)

Today at 3:00 P.M. local time, Americans traditionally take a minute to honor U.S. veterans who have died in action.

26 *Tuesday*

If the hem of a lady's skirt turns up to form a pocket, good fortune may come her way soon.

27 *Wednesday*

The human mind always makes progress, but it is a progress in spirals.
—Madame de Staël, French writer (1766–1817)

28 *Thursday*

If kites fly high, fine weather is at hand.

MAY • 2009   JUNE • 2009

S	M	T	W	T	F	S		S	M	T	W	T	F	S
					1	2			1	2	3	4	5	6
3	4	5	6	7	8	9		7	8	9	10	11	12	13
10	11	12	13	14	15	16		14	15	16	17	18	19	20
17	18	19	20	21	22	23		21	22	23	24	25	26	27
24	25	26	27	28	29	30		28	29	30				
31														

Friday **29**

To wash paint off
sensitive skin, rub
with lard or vegetable
shortening, wait a few
minutes, and wipe off.

Saturday **30**

First Quarter

Gnats galore,
screen the door.
-The Old Farmer's Almanac, *1977*

Sunday **31**

Whitsunday—Pentecost

To keep your true love,
put marigolds in your
wedding bouquet.

REMINDERS

....

....

....

....

....

Complement this calendar with daily weather and Almanac wit and wisdom at Almanac.com.

MONTHLY REMINDERS

Why is June 13, 1983, an important day in astronomy's history?

That's the day on which the U.S. space probe *Pioneer 10* became the first man-made object to leave the solar system.

What's Your Sign?

GEMINI

MAY 21–JUNE 20

Symbol: Ⅱ *The Twins*
Ruling planet: *Mercury*
Element: *Air*
Quality: *The intellect*
Ability: *Writing and communications*
Traits: *Mercurial, expressive, lighthearted*

Full Strawberry Moon

This month's full Moon was celebrated by the Algonquin tribes as a time to gather ripening fruit. It is also called the Rose Moon and the Hot Moon.

To Your Health

Can't sleep? Try these tips for a restful night:

Sleep and wake on a regular schedule. Don't sleep late to make up for a late night. Avoid napping during the day, unless necessary.

Cut out the caffeine, at least after lunch. Avoid coffee, chocolate, and caffeinated sodas or tea.

Exercise in the late afternoon. It can help to deepen sleep stages at night.

Plan a relaxing routine just before bedtime. Soak in a tub.

Listen to soft music or do some light reading.

Skip the alcohol at night. Initially, it can act as a sedative, but it can disrupt sleep later on that evening.

Don't drink or eat too much before going to bed, and avoid spicy dinners.

AGE-OLD ADVICE

The young man who is in the habit of early rising, will and must be in the habit of retiring early, and, of course, will put himself out of the way of many temptations and dangers which come under the veil of midnight.

–Rev. John Todd, The Student's Manual, *1854*

Cut your thistles before St. John [June 24], You will have two instead of one.

The best hay is just dried grass, cut when it is full of juice. It is sweet then, and you will see that the cows will take hold of it, and look and act as if they wanted to say that it went just to the right place.

–The Old Farmer's Almanac, June 1884

JUNE

1 *Monday*

The Aztecs used cocoa beans as currency. A rabbit cost ten beans.

2 *Tuesday*

Everyone has a unique set of teeth— even identical twins.

3 *Wednesday*

Remedy for hiccups: Lay a broom on the floor, bristles to the right, and jump over it seven times.

4 *Thursday*

Q: What is smarter than a hummingbird? A: A spelling bee.

JUNE • 2009   JULY • 2009

S	M	T	W	T	F	S
	1	2	3	4	5	6
7	8	9	10	11	12	13
14	15	16	17	18	19	20
21	22	23	24	25	26	27
28	29	30				

S	M	T	W	T	F	S
			1	2	3	4
5	6	7	8	9	10	11
12	13	14	15	16	17	18
19	20	21	22	23	24	25
26	27	28	29	30	31	

World Environment Day

Friday

5

*Behold the world, how
it is whirled round,
And for it is so whirl'd,
is named so.*

–Sir John Davies, English poet
(1569–1626)

Today is a good day
to go camping.

Saturday

6

Orthodox Pentecost
Full Strawberry Moon

Sunday

7

Suspend netting over
strawberries to deter
birds.

REMINDERS

....
....
....
....
....
....

JUNE

8 *Monday*

To have wholesome cooking, however good the food purchased, the cook must be cheerful and enjoy the work.
—Mary Elizabeth Carter, American writer

9 *Tuesday*

Going on an ocean cruise? Toss a penny overboard for good luck.

10 *Wednesday*

Bees will not swarm
Before a near storm.

11 *Thursday*

King Kamehameha I Day
(Hawaii)

Hawaii is the only U.S. state that was once a kingdom with its own monarchy.

JUNE • 2009 JULY • 2009

S	M	T	W	T	F	S
	1	2	3	4	5	6
7	8	9	10	11	12	13
14	15	16	17	18	19	20
21	22	23	24	25	26	27
28	29	30				

S	M	T	W	T	F	S
			1	2	3	4
5	6	7	8	9	10	11
12	13	14	15	16	17	18
19	20	21	22	23	24	25
26	27	28	29	30	31	

Friday 12

If a crop wilts
readily, check for
galls (swellings or
knots) on the roots—
a sign of root-knot
nematodes.

Saturday 13

*Proud Papa and
tearful Mater greet the
grinning graduater.*
—The Old Farmer's
Almanac, *1994*

Flag Day *Sunday* 14

When the U.S. flag
is displayed in a
window, position the
blue union so that it
is in the upper left
as observed from
the street.

REMINDERS

....
....
....
....
....

JUNE

15 Monday

Last Quarter

On this day in 1970, soccer player Amanda Cromwell was born.

16 Tuesday

Install a motion-activated sprinkler to discourage animals from exploring your garden.

17 Wednesday

Bunker Hill Day
(Suffolk Co., Mass.)

The Battle of Bunker Hill was fought mainly on Breed's Hill.

18 Thursday

The greatest right in the world is the right to be wrong.

—Harry Weinberger, American lawyer (1888–1944)

JUNE • 2009

S	M	T	W	T	F	S
	1	2	3	4	5	6
7	8	9	10	11	12	13
14	15	16	17	18	19	20
21	22	23	24	25	26	27
28	29	30				

JULY • 2009

S	M	T	W	T	F	S
			1	2	3	4
5	6	7	8	9	10	11
12	13	14	15	16	17	18
19	20	21	22	23	24	25
26	27	28	29	30	31	

Emancipation Day (Tex.)

Friday 19

Tongue twister:
The sixth sick sheik's
sixth sheep's sick.

West Virginia Day

Saturday 20

Today is a good day
to end old projects.

Father's Day
National Aboriginal Day
(Canada)
Summer Solstice

Sunday 21

Venus has the longest
day in our solar
system—243 Earth
days long!

REMINDERS

....

....

....

....

....

JUNE

22 *Monday*

New Moon

If mists in the new Moon, rain in the old.

23 *Tuesday*

Delphinium comes from a Greek word for "dolphin," because the flower buds resemble a dolphin's head.

24 *Wednesday*

Discovery Day (N.L., Can.)
Fête Nationale (Qué., Can.)

On this day in 1497, explorer John Cabot landed on "new found land."

25 *Thursday*

A calico cat usually ha a fair amount of white with distinct patches of red and black.

JUNE • 2009

S	M	T	W	T	F	S
	1	2	3	4	5	6
7	8	9	10	11	12	13
14	15	16	17	18	19	20
21	22	23	24	25	26	27
28	29	30				

JULY • 2009

S	M	T	W	T	F	S
			1	2	3	4
5	6	7	8	9	10	11
12	13	14	15	16	17	18
19	20	21	22	23	24	25
26	27	28	29	30	31	

To deter fruit flies,
store fresh fruit in
closed containers or
the refrigerator.

Friday **26**

*Reality reveals
itself only when it is
illuminated by a
ray of poetry.*
*−Georges Braque, French artist
(1882–1963)*

Saturday **27**

Married in the
merry month of June,
Life will be one
honeymoon.

Sunday **28**

REMINDERS

....
....
....
....
....
....

29 Monday

First Quarter

A dream about filberts signifies peace and harmony.

30 Tuesday

It's very hard to take yourself too seriously when you look at the world from outer space.
–Thomas K. Mattingly II,
Apollo 16 *astronaut (b. 1936)*

1 Wednesday

Canada Day

The Philadelphia Zoo, which opened on this day in 1874, was the first public zoo in the United States.

2 Thursday

When eating soup, hold your spoon like a pencil and dip away from you.

JUNE • 2009

S	M	T	W	T	F	S
	1	2	3	4	5	6
7	8	9	10	11	12	13
14	15	16	17	18	19	20
21	22	23	24	25	26	27
28	29	30				

JULY • 2009

S	M	T	W	T	F	S
			1	2	3	4
5	6	7	8	9	10	11
12	13	14	15	16	17	18
19	20	21	22	23	24	25
26	27	28	29	30	31	

Friday

3

Sirius A, the brightest star at night, is named the Dog Star because it shines in the constellation Canis Major (Big Dog).

Saturday

4

Independence Day

. . . we mutually pledge to each other our lives, our fortunes, and our sacred honor.

–Declaration of Independence, *1776*

Sunday

5

To control Japanese beetles, pluck them off plants and drop them into a bucket of soapy water.

REMINDERS

MONTHLY REMINDERS

How many people signed the Declaration of Independence?

56. Edward Rutledge from South Carolina was the youngest, at 26, and Benjamin Franklin from Pennsylvania was the oldest, at 70.

What's Your Sign?

CANCER
JUNE 21–JULY 22

Symbol: ♋ *The Crab*
Ruling planet: *Moon*
Element: *Water*
Quality: *Sensitivity*
Ability: *Nurturing*
Traits: *Compassionate, domestic, protective*

Full Buck Moon

To Your Health

One way to minimize your total blood cholesterol is to manage the amount and types of fat in your diet. Aim for monounsaturated and polyunsaturated fats; avoid saturated and trans fats.

Monounsaturated fat lowers LDL (bad cholesterol) and may raise HDL (good cholesterol) or leave it unchanged. Found in almonds, avocados, canola oil, cashews, olive oil, peanut oil, and peanuts.

Polyunsaturated fat lowers LDL and may lower HDL. Includes omega-3 and omega-6 fatty acids. Found in corn oil, cottonseed oil, fish such as salmon and tuna, safflower oil, sesame seeds, soybeans, and sunflower oil.

Saturated fat raises both LDL and HDL. Found in chocolate, cocoa butter, coconut oil, dairy products (milk, butter, cheese, ice cream), egg yolks, palm oil, and red meat.

Trans fat raises LDL and lowers HDL. A type of fat common in many processed foods, such as most margarines (especially stick), vegetable shortening, partially hydrogenated vegetable oil, many commercial fried foods (doughnuts, french fries), and commercial baked goods (cookies, crackers, cakes).

This month's full Moon is so named because it occurs during the time when bucks begin growing antlers. It is also known as the Thunder Moon.

No tempest, good July,
Lest the corn look ruely.

AGE-OLD ADVICE

If persons eat much fat they must have more fresh air to burn it. A person confined to the house needs to be careful what fats, and how much, are taken.

–Margaret E. Dodd, Chemistry of the Household, *1912*

*G*ood water, and plenty of it, is one of the first things to look out for on the farm and everywhere else. The health of man and beast depends upon it.

–The Old Farmer's Almanac, July 1884

JULY

6   *Monday*

It is easier to
separate the yolk
from the white if the
egg is cold.

7   *Tuesday*

Full Buck Moon

A group of trout is
called a hover.

8   *Wednesday*

Tomatoes with dark,
leathery patches at the
bottom may have
blossom end rot, due
to a lack of calcium
uptake.

9   *Thursday*

Nunavut Day (Canada)

*Keep your faith in
all beautiful things; in
the Sun when it is
hidden, in the Spring
when it is gone.*
–Roy R. Gilson, American write
(1875–1933

JULY • 2009   AUGUST • 2009

S	M	T	W	T	F	S
			1	2	3	4
5	6	7	8	9	10	11
12	13	14	15	16	17	18
19	20	21	22	23	24	25
26	27	28	29	30	31	

S	M	T	W	T	F	S
						1
2	3	4	5	6	7	8
9	10	11	12	13	14	15
16	17	18	19	20	21	22
23	24	25	26	27	28	29
30	31					

Friday 10

If it rains on July 10, it will rain for seven weeks.

Saturday 11

Planning a big gathering? Four quarts of ice cream will serve about 25 people.

Sunday 12

Orangemen's Day (N.L., Can.)

On this day in 1730, potter Josiah Wedgwood was born.

REMINDERS

July

13 *Monday*

Clean a manual can opener by feeding a paper towel through it.

14 *Tuesday*

Either you decide to stay in the shallow end of the pool or you go out in the ocean.
–Christopher Reeve, American actor (1952–2004)

15 *Wednesday*

Last Quarter

Today is a good day to destroy pests and weeds.

16 *Thursday*

Enjoy the warm before the storm.
–The Old Farmer's Almanac, *1972*

JULY • 2009   AUGUST • 2009

S	M	T	W	T	F	S
			1	2	3	4
5	6	7	8	9	10	11
12	13	14	15	16	17	18
19	20	21	22	23	24	25
26	27	28	29	30	31	

S	M	T	W	T	F	S
						1
2	3	4	5	6	7	8
9	10	11	12	13	14	15
16	17	18	19	20	21	22
23	24	25	26	27	28	29
30	31					

Friday 17

Baptisia comes from a Greek word for "dye," because the plant was used to make a substitute for indigo.

Saturday 18

Dream of a pen and you will be gifted with knowledge.

Sunday 19

I hate to spread rumors, but what else can one do with them?
–Amanda Lear, French entertainer (b. 1946)

REMINDERS

....
....
....
....
....

July

20 *Monday*

Blue eyes indicate
a meek and gentle
temper.

21 *Tuesday*

New Moon

**The more laws,
the more offenses.**

22 *Wednesday*

*Memory is the
treasury and guardian
of all things.*
–Cicero, Latin philosopher
(106–43 B.C.)

23 *Thursday*

Lightning helps
to convert a small
percentage of nitrogen
in the air to a form
that plants can use.

JULY • 2009

S M T W T F S
          1 2 3 4
5 6 7 8 9 10 11
12 13 14 15 16 17 18
19 20 21 22 23 24 25
26 27 28 29 30 31

AUGUST • 2009

S M T W T F S
                1
2 3 4 5 6 7 8
9 10 11 12 13 14 15
16 17 18 19 20 21 22
23 24 25 26 27 28 29
30 31

Friday **24**

Pioneer Day (Utah)

Legend claims that
a town in the middle
of Utah was named
Levan because it spells
"navel" backwards.

Saturday **25**

Today is a good day
to harvest
aboveground crops.

Sunday **26**

Men and pyramids
are not made to stand on
their heads.

REMINDERS

July ❧ August

27 *Monday*

Place sprigs of
summer savory in
drawers to repel
moths.

28 *Tuesday*

First Quarter

No sweet without sweat.

29 *Wednesday*

Soothe a sunburn
with buttermilk.

30 *Thursday*

Words are like bees:
They have honey and
a sting.

JULY • 2009   AUGUST • 2009

S M T W T F S   S M T W T F S
        1 2 3 4   1
5 6 7 8 9 10 11   2 3 4 5 6 7 8
12 13 14 15 16 17 18   9 10 11 12 13 14 15
19 20 21 22 23 24 25   16 17 18 19 20 21 22
26 27 28 29 30 31   23 24 25 26 27 28 29
                    30 31

Friday 31

Plant a second crop
of lettuce in the shade
of tomato plants
or under cucumber
vines.

Saturday 1

**If you would avoid
suspicion, don't lace your
shoes in a melon field.**
—Chinese proverb

Sunday 2

*Oh! What a crowded
world one moment
may contain!*
*—Felicia Dorothea Hemans,
English poet (1793–1835)*

REMINDERS

MONTHLY REMINDERS

What is the fastest fish?

Although this is hard to measure in the wild, it's said that the honor goes to the sailfish, which has been clocked at approximately 68 miles per hour over a short period of time.

What's Your Sign?

LEO

JULY 23–AUGUST 22

Symbol: ♌ *The Lion*
Ruling planet: *Sun*
Element: *Fire*
Quality: *Dramatic*
Ability: *Natural leadership*
Traits: *Charming, forceful, ambitious*

To Your Health

Want to minimize future wrinkles?
Take care of your skin!

🕭 Avoid unnecessary exposure to direct sunlight. Do not sunbathe or use sunlamps or tanning beds. Stay out of the sun between 10 A.M. and 4 P.M.

🕭 Apply sunscreen every day, all year. Apply 20 minutes before going outside and repeat every 2 hours; also reapply after swimming or exercising. Choose a sunscreen that has UVA and UVB protection and a minimum SPF of 15.

🕭 Wear protective clothing—long sleeves, wide-brim hat, and sunglasses with UV protection.

🕭 Do not smoke.

🕭 Exercise daily and eat a healthy diet. Include foods high in antioxidants. Drink at least six to eight glasses of water a day. Avoid alcohol.

🕭 Get plenty of sleep. Sleep on your back.

🕭 Moisturize your skin regularly.

AGE-OLD ADVICE

Face veils have, perhaps, more to do with affecting the complexion than you may think . . . . Red is the best to keep off freckles. Reddish brown stands next in line.

–Dr. Emma E. Walker, Beauty and Health, *1904*

Full Sturgeon Moon

This month's full Moon got its name because the sturgeon of the Great Lakes and Lake Champlain were most readily caught at this time. It is also called the Green Corn Moon and the Red Moon.

🕭

August sunshine and bright nights ripen the grapes.

---

*P*ick early pears, to ripen in the house.

–The Old Farmer's Almanac, August 1884

AUGUST

3 *Monday*

Colorado Day
Civic Holiday (Canada)

*Q: What did the
beach say when the
tide came in?*
A: Long time, no sea.

4 *Tuesday*

The North Star,
Polaris, is the last star
in the handle of the
Little Dipper.

5 *Wednesday*

Full Sturgeon Moon

When camping, avoid
scented shampoos or
perfumes—they
attract mosquitoes!

6 *Thursday*

Never stop a running horse
to give it sugar.

AUGUST • 2009

S	M	T	W	T	F	S
						1
2	3	4	5	6	7	8
9	10	11	12	13	14	15
16	17	18	19	20	21	22
23	24	25	26	27	28	29
30	31					

SEPTEMBER • 2009

S	M	T	W	T	F	S
		1	2	3	4	5
6	7	8	9	10	11	12
13	14	15	16	17	18	19
20	21	22	23	24	25	26
27	28	29	30			

Friday 7

To strengthen your nails, soak them in warm olive oil for five minutes.

Saturday 8

In spite of their name, yardlong beans are best harvested when their pods are between 12 and 15 inches long.

Sunday 9

To make a fine gentleman, several trades are required, but chiefly a barber.

–Oliver Goldsmith, British poet
(1730–74)

REMINDERS

....
....
....
....
....
....

Complement this calendar with daily weather and Almanac wit and wisdom at Almanac.com.

AUGUST

10 *Monday*

On this day in 1874, President Herbert Hoover was born.

11 *Tuesday*

Today is a good day to cut hay.

12 *Wednesday*

Big doesn't necessarily mean better. Sunflowers aren't better than violets.

–Edna Ferber, American writer
(1887–1968)

13 *Thursday*

Last Quarter

The best fish swims near the bottom.

AUGUST • 2009   SEPTEMBER • 2009

S	M	T	W	T	F	S
						1
2	3	4	5	6	7	8
9	10	11	12	13	14	15
16	17	18	19	20	21	22
23	24	25	26	27	28	29
30	31					

S	M	T	W	T	F	S
		1	2	3	4	5
6	7	8	9	10	11	12
13	14	15	16	17	18	19
20	21	22	23	24	25	26
27	28	29	30			

As long as the Sun shines, one does not ask for the Moon.
—Russian proverb

Friday 14

Zinnia was named after Johann Gottfried Zinn, an 18th-century German botany professor.

Saturday 15

Bennington Battle Day (Vt.)

Be not simply good; be good for something.
—Henry David Thoreau,
American writer (1817–62)

Sunday 16

REMINDERS

AUGUST

17 Monday

Discovery Day (Y.T., Can.)

If you are going to be whistling, avoid waxy lip products; they tend to distort the tone.

18 Tuesday

Vision is the art of seeing things invisible.
–Jonathan Swift, English satirist (1667–1745)

19 Wednesday

National Aviation Day

To relieve a minor burn, apply a paste of ground cabbage leaves and water to the affected area for 30 to 60 minutes.

20 Thursday

New Moon

The Earth is a beehive we all enter by the same door but live in different cells.
–African prove

AUGUST • 2009   SEPTEMBER • 2009

S	M	T	W	T	F	S
						1
2	3	4	5	6	7	8
9	10	11	12	13	14	15
16	17	18	19	20	21	22
23	24	25	26	27	28	29
30	31					

S	M	T	W	T	F	S
		1	2	3	4	5
6	7	8	9	10	11	12
13	14	15	16	17	18	19
20	21	22	23	24	25	26
27	28	29	30			

Friday 21

The first hospital ambulance service was introduced in Cincinnati, Ohio, around 1865.

Saturday 22

First day of Ramadan

A well-stored mind is the first requisite to a happy and useful life.
–The Old Farmer's Almanac, *1873*

Sunday 23

Set the mowing height on your mower to 2 or 3 inches. Taller grass fares better during a dry spell.

REMINDERS

AUGUST

24 *Monday*

No pear falls into a
shut mouth.
–Italian proverb

25 *Tuesday*

Put rice grains
in your fishing tackle
box to absorb
moisture and prevent
rusty hooks.

26 *Wednesday*

Women's Equality Day

*Being a woman is a
terribly difficult trade,
since it consists
principally of dealing
with men.*
*–Joseph Conrad, Ukrainian-born
English writer (1857–1924)*

27 *Thursday*

First Quarter

To cure a headache,
place a buckwheat
cake on your head.

AUGUST • 2009

S	M	T	W	T	F	S
						1
2	3	4	5	6	7	8
9	10	11	12	13	14	15
16	17	18	19	20	21	22
23	24	25	26	27	28	29
30	31					

SEPTEMBER • 2009

S	M	T	W	T	F	S
		1	2	3	4	5
6	7	8	9	10	11	12
13	14	15	16	17	18	19
20	21	22	23	24	25	26
27	28	29	30			

Friday **28**

Lots of gnats and flies around the compost pile may indicate that it needs more aeration.

Saturday **29**

Art is I; science is we.
–Claude Bernard, French
physiologist (1813–78)

Sunday **30**

Today is a good day to set posts or pour concrete.

R EMINDERS

....
....
....
....
....
....
....

Complement this calendar with daily weather and Almanac wit and wisdom at Almanac.com.

31 *Monday*

Fleas can jump
150 times their own
length, vertically or
horizontally.

1 *Tuesday*

Add 1 teaspoon
of baking powder to
1 cup of hot water.
If the mixture doesn't
bubble, the baking
powder is too old
to use.

2 *Wednesday*

*Today's mighty oak
is yesterday's nut that
held its ground.*

–Rosa Parks, American civil rights
activist (1931–2005)

3 *Thursday*

To clean a plastic
shower curtain, wipe
it with a mixture of
equal parts white
vinegar and water.

AUGUST • 2009

S	M	T	W	T	F	S
						1
2	3	4	5	6	7	8
9	10	11	12	13	14	15
16	17	18	19	20	21	22
23	24	25	26	27	28	29
30	31					

SEPTEMBER • 2009

S	M	T	W	T	F	S
		1	2	3	4	5
6	7	8	9	10	11	12
13	14	15	16	17	18	19
20	21	22	23	24	25	26
27	28	29	30			

Full Corn Moon

Friday 4

The thought has good legs, and the quill a good tongue.
—*English proverb*

Saturday 5

Move potted half-hardy perennial plants to an unheated garage or basement before the first fall frost.

Sunday 6

Around 1889, before football helmets, some teams wore their hair long as "protection" from head injuries.

REMINDERS

SEPTEMBER with *The Old Farmer's Almanac*

ASK THE ALMANAC

Who wrote the melody for the song "Happy Birthday to You"?

Kindergarten teacher Mildred J. Hill wrote the music in 1893. Her sister, Patty Smith Hill, wrote the lyrics. The song, titled "Good Morning to All," was meant to be used by teachers to greet their students. The melody is copyright-protected even now.

What's Your Sign?

VIRGO

AUGUST 23–SEPTEMBER 22

Symbol: ♍ *The Virgin*
Ruling planet: *Mercury*
Element: *Earth*
Quality: *Logical*
Ability: *To reason*
Traits: *Analytical, neat, dependable*

Full Great Corn Moon

To Your Health

Here are a few ways to pump up your brainpower:

🐦 Read, read, read. Reading is the number one brain-boosting activity.

🐦 Eat brain-boosting foods. Salmon, sardines, and tuna are rich in omega-3 fatty acids, which are essential to healthy brain function. Blueberries help to neutralize oxidizing free radicals that may contribute to age-related diseases after long-term exposure. Liver is an excellent source of B vitamins, necessary for alertness, memory, and learning. Spinach is a good source of antioxidant vitamins E and C and contains the B vitamin folic acid.

🐦 Vary your daily routine: Brush your teeth with your nondominant hand. Take an unfamiliar route to work. In your office, reposition items that you use often, such as your wastebasket. When you get home, try to locate the correct door key by sense of touch.

This month's full Moon got its name for the ripe corn ready to be picked. It is also known as the Barley Moon.

🐦

Heavy September rains bring drought.

*I*t is high time to cut up corn for the silo.

–The Old Farmer's Almanac, *September 1884*

AGE-OLD ADVICE

Mental food must be digested before it can give strength to our minds.

–Mrs. Henry Mackarness, editor, The Young Lady's Book, *1876*

September

7 *Monday*

Labor Day

Worry is a misuse of the imagination.

–Dan Zadra, American
writer (b. 1946)

8 *Tuesday*

The *2010 Old
Farmer's Almanac*
officially goes on
sale today.

9 *Wednesday*

Admission Day (Calif.)

San Bernardino
County in California
is the largest county
by area (20,160
square miles) in the
contiguous United
States.

10 *Thursday*

*Sun dapples apples;
showers hit and miss.
What could be sweeter
than days like this?*

–The Old Farmer's Almanac, 1987

SEPTEMBER • 2009

S	M	T	W	T	F	S
		1	2	3	4	5
6	7	8	9	10	11	12
13	14	15	16	17	18	19
20	21	22	23	24	25	26
27	28	29	30			

OCTOBER • 2009

S	M	T	W	T	F	S
				1	2	3
4	5	6	7	8	9	10
11	12	13	14	15	16	17
18	19	20	21	22	23	24
25	26	27	28	29	30	31

Friday

11

Patriot Day
Last Quarter

☆ ☆

Deodorize a thermos
with salt water.

Saturday

12

*It takes less time to do
a thing right than to
explain why you did
it wrong.*

–Henry Wadsworth Longfellow,
American poet (1807–82)

Sunday

13

Grandparents Day

Time gives good advice.

–Maltese proverb

REMINDERS

....

....

....

....

....

Complement this calendar with daily weather and Almanac wit and wisdom at Almanac.com.

September

14 *Monday*

Today is a good day to can, pickle, or make sauerkraut.

15 *Tuesday*

On the Moon, you'd weigh less than 20 percent of your current weight.

16 *Wednesday*

Plant spring bulbs, such as narcissus, snowdrop, and winter aconite, before the ground freezes.

17 *Thursday*

Constitution Day

Society is the union of men and not the men themselves.

–Charles Louis de Secondat Montesquieu, French philosopher (1689–175

SEPTEMBER • 2009	OCTOBER • 2009
S M T W T F S	S M T W T F S
1 2 3 4 5	1 2 3
6 7 8 9 10 11 12	4 5 6 7 8 9 10
13 14 15 16 17 18 19	11 12 13 14 15 16 17
20 21 22 23 24 25 26	18 19 20 21 22 23 24
27 28 29 30	25 26 27 28 29 30 31

New Moon

Friday **18**

Two captains will
sink the ship.

—Turkish proverb

Rosh Hashanah

Saturday **19**

On Rosh Hashanah,
Jews eat challah
dipped in honey
to symbolize
sweetness and good
fortune to come.

Sunday **20**

After steam cleaning a
carpet, turn up the
heat or open windows
and use fans to speed
up the drying process.

REMINDERS

....
....
....
....
....

September

21 Monday

International Day of Peace

Salvia comes from a Latin word meaning to "save" or "heal," referring to the medicinal qualities of some species.

22 Tuesday

Autumnal Equinox

Sweet and smiling are thy ways, Beauteous, golden Autumn days.

–Will Carleton, American poet
(1845–1912)

23 Wednesday

To keep iceberg lettuce crisp, wrap it in a moist paper towel, place in a perforated plastic bag, and store in the crisper drawer of the refrigerator.

24 Thursday

On this day in 1896, writer F. Scott Fitzgerald was born.

SEPTEMBER • 2009

S	M	T	W	T	F	S
		1	2	3	4	5
6	7	8	9	10	11	12
13	14	15	16	17	18	19
20	21	22	23	24	25	26
27	28	29	30			

OCTOBER • 2009

S	M	T	W	T	F	S
				1	2	3
4	5	6	7	8	9	10
11	12	13	14	15	16	17
18	19	20	21	22	23	24
25	26	27	28	29	30	31

Friday 25

*From middle age on,
everything of interest is
either illegal, immoral,
or fattening.*

–Alexander Woollcott, American
writer (1887–1943)

Saturday 26

First Quarter

When beechnuts
are plentiful, expect a
mild winter.

Sunday 27

Today is a good day
to harvest
aboveground crops.

REMINDERS

....

....

....

....

....

....

September ❧ October

28 Monday

Yom Kippur

The only man who never makes a mistake is the man who never does anything.

—Theodore Roosevelt, 26th U.S. president (1858–1919)

29 Tuesday

Well lathered is half shaven.

30 Wednesday

The secret of education is respecting the pupil.

—Ralph Waldo Emerson, American writer (1803–82)

1 Thursday

One hundred nine Earths would fit across the Sun's diameter.

The Easiest Thing You'll Do All Year!

How would you like to receive next year's elegant Engagement Calendar PLUS a copy of *The Old Farmer's Almanac* AND save the hassle of reordering?

Order your 2010 calendar today, and join our **Special No-Hassle Renewal Program:** Each year, we'll reserve your copy of The Old Farmer's Almanac Engagement Calendar, PLUS that year's edition of *The Old Farmer's Almanac* as our gift to you. We'll send you an advance notice of shipment as a reminder, and include a postage-paid reply card in case you have changes to your address or quantity, or wish to cancel your order. If you choose to receive your new calendar, you won't have to do a thing—we'll mail it (and your Almanac) in early September, along with your invoice.

You may cancel this program at any time with no further obligation, and will always have 30 days to respond to our reminder.

Order today, and we'll rush your 2010 Engagement Calendar to your doorstep and sign you up for our Special No-Hassle Renewal Program. Why wait ? It's that easy!

FREE ALMANAC with your order a $5.99 value!

Due to mailing requirements, we regret that we are unable to offer this program outside of the United States.

THREE EASY WAYS TO ORDER

 Online Shop.Almanac.com

 Mail Cut out, complete, and fold this form, tape and mail.
Or, use your own envelope and mail to the address on the back of this form.

🕿 **Phone** Toll-free 1-800-ALMANAC, mention key A79EEC.

ORDERED BY:

_____
Name

_____
Address

_____
City / State / Zip

2010 calendars are scheduled to ship beginning in September 2009.

ORDER SUMMARY:

____ copies SPECIAL RENEWAL OF10CEGC @ $14.99 $_____

Massachusetts (5%) or Illinois (6.25%) Sales Tax $_____

+ Shipping and Handling $ 4.95

Key code: A79EEC TOTAL ENCLOSED: $_____

☐ Bill me

☐ Check or money order enclosed

Charge my: ☐ Visa   ☐ MasterCard
☐ American Express ☐ Discover/NOVUS

_____
Account Number   Exp. Date

_____
Signature (required for credit card orders)

A79EEC

For fastest service, go to Shop.Almanac.com

Name: _____

Address: _____

_____

City/Town: _____ State: _____ Zip: _____

 RUSH!

*Order
for 2010
calendar
enclosed!*

- -

Fold along this line. ⬆

After cutting this order form out of the book along vertical dotted line, fold in half along horizontal dotted line. Please be sure to either complete the credit card information on the order form or enclose a check. Then tape the envelope closed along the three open edges. Do not send cash.

Cut along this line. ⬇

Use clear tape on all three open sides to seal completely.

October

OCTOBER • 2009

S M T W T F S
1 2 3
4 5 6 7 8 9 10
11 12 13 14 15 16 17
18 19 20 21 22 23 24
25 26 27 28 29 30 31

NOVEMBER • 2009

S M T W T F S
1 2 3 4 5 6 7
8 9 10 11 12 13 14
15 16 17 18 19 20 21
22 23 24 25 26 27 28
29 30

A good song is none the worse for being sung twice.

Friday

2

The ostrich has the largest eyes of any land animal—each up to 2 inches across.

Saturday

3

Full Harvest Moon

For best results, harvest crops during a waning Moon.

Sunday

4

REMINDERS

....
....
....
....
....

OCTOBER with *The Old Farmer's Almanac*

MONTHLY REMINDERS

_____
_____
_____
_____
_____
_____
_____
_____
_____
_____
_____
_____
_____
_____
_____
_____
_____
_____
_____
_____
_____
_____

ASK THE ALMANAC

Who owned the first Akita dog in the United States?

Helen Keller. In 1937, during a lecture tour in Japan, she expressed an interest in owning one of the dogs. She was later presented with a puppy named Kamikaze-Go, which became the first Akita dog to reside in United States.

What's Your Sign?

LIBRA

SEPTEMBER 23–OCTOBER 22

Symbol: ♎ *The Scales*
Ruling planet: *Venus*
Element: *Air*
Quality: *Empathy*
Ability: *Diplomacy*
Traits: *Tactful, artistic, sociable*

Full Harvest Moon

*The Harvest Moon is always
the full Moon nearest the
autumnal equinox, delivering
more light in the evening to aid
in the harvest.*

*Dry your barley in October,
Or you'll always be sober.*

> All fruits that are worth
> much ought to be picked
> by hand.
>
> –The Old Farmer's Almanac, *October 1884*

To Your Health

Stressed out? Here are some exercises to help you relax.

DEEP BREATHING

Breathe from your abdomen, not your chest. Slowly take in a deep breath through your nose; you should feel your stomach expand. Then exhale slowly through your mouth, getting rid of all of the air in your lungs. Repeat until you feel calmer.

PROGRESSIVE MUSCLE RELAXATION (PMR)

Lie down or sit in a comfortable chair. Close your eyes. Focus on your toes; tense the muscles for a few seconds and then relax them. Move on upward through your body, tensing and then releasing the muscles in each section, until all parts of your body are relaxed.

VISUALIZATION

Sit or lie down. Close your eyes. Picture yourself in a peaceful place. Think about the sights, sounds, fragrances, textures, temperature, and so forth. Focus on this place until you feel relaxed and then gradually return to the present with those peaceful feelings.

AGE-OLD ADVICE

*The mind that attains the habit of throwing off study
and anxiety, and relaxing itself at once, has obtained
 treasure.*

–Rev. John Todd, The Student's Manual, *1854*

October

5 Monday

Pretty much all of the honest truthtelling there is in the world is done by children.
—Oliver Wendell Holmes, American writer (1809–94)

6 Tuesday

Aster comes from a Greek word for "star," because of the flower's shape.

7 Wednesday

Seasoned wood should show cracks at the ends and make a sharp "thunk" when hit against another log.

8 Thursday

During fall, interior (older) needles of pines, spruces, and firs normally turn yellow or brown and drop off.

OCTOBER • 2009

S	M	T	W	T	F	S
				1	2	3
4	5	6	7	8	9	10
11	12	13	14	15	16	17
18	19	20	21	22	23	24
25	26	27	28	29	30	31

NOVEMBER • 2009

S	M	T	W	T	F	S
1	2	3	4	5	6	7
8	9	10	11	12	13	14
15	16	17	18	19	20	21
22	23	24	25	26	27	28
29	30					

Leif Eriksson Day

Friday **9**

*It's a joy to gaze
On these beautiful days.*
–The Old Farmer's Almanac, *1955*

On this day in 1958, country singer Tanya Tucker was born.

Saturday **10**

Last Quarter

Sunday **11**

Unwashed mushrooms will keep best if refrigerated in a paper bag.

REMINDERS

....
....
....
....
....

OCTOBER

12 Monday

Columbus Day (observed)
Thanksgiving Day
(Canada)

Columbus's favorite
ship, *Santa Clara,* was
owned by Juan
Niño—hence its nick-
name, *Niña.*

13 Tuesday

Drink warm lemonade
to reduce a fever.

14 Wednesday

*Birds sing after a
storm; why shouldn't
people feel as free to
delight in whatever
remains to them?*

–Rose Fitzgerald Kennedy, American matriarch (1890–1995)

15 Thursday

In October dung your field,
And your land its wealth
shall yield.

OCTOBER • 2009

S	M	T	W	T	F	S
				1	2	3
4	5	6	7	8	9	10
11	12	13	14	15	16	17
18	19	20	21	22	23	24
25	26	27	28	29	30	31

NOVEMBER • 2009

S	M	T	W	T	F	S
1	2	3	4	5	6	7
8	9	10	11	12	13	14
15	16	17	18	19	20	21
22	23	24	25	26	27	28
29	30					

A baby giraffe
is about
6 feet tall
at birth.

Friday 16

Today is a good day to
end old projects.

Saturday 17

Alaska Day
New Moon

Sunday 18

About one-third of
Alaska is within the
Arctic Circle.

REMINDERS

....
....
....
....
....

Complement this calendar with daily weather and Almanac wit and wisdom at Almanac.com.

OCTOBER

19 *Monday*

To best get rid of germs, wash your hands for at least 20 seconds once lathere

20 *Tuesday*

Far burr [halo around the Moon], near rain.

21 *Wednesday*

When you reach for the stars you may no quite get one, but yo won't come up with a handful of mud eithe

—Leo Burnett, Americ businessman (1891–197

22 *Thursday*

Can't sleep? Drink chamomile te

OCTOBER • 2009

S	M	T	W	T	F	S
				1	2	3
4	5	6	7	8	9	10
11	12	13	14	15	16	17
18	19	20	21	22	23	24
25	26	27	28	29	30	31

NOVEMBER • 2009

S	M	T	W	T	F	S
1	2	3	4	5	6	7
8	9	10	11	12	13	14
15	16	17	18	19	20	21
22	23	24	25	26	27	28
29	30					

Friday 23

Carrying an acorn in your pocket will keep you young

Saturday 24

United Nations Day

Light is the task when many share the toil.
–Homer, Greek epic poet (9th–8th cent. B.C.)

Sunday 25

First Quarter

A little soap on the hinges will remedy a creaky door.

REMINDERS

Complement this calendar with daily weather and Almanac wit and wisdom at Almanac.com.

26 *Monday*

For good luck, always remove the right shoe before the left.

27 *Tuesday*

Moose can run up to about 35 miles per hour.

28 *Wednesday*

Sleep hath its own world,
And a wide realm of wild reality.

–Lord George Gordon Byron,
English poet (1788–1824)

29 *Thursday*

When *The House of the Seven Gables* was published in 1851, the actual Salem, Massachusetts, home had only three of the original seven gables.

OCTOBER • 2009

S	M	T	W	T	F	S
				1	2	3
4	5	6	7	8	9	10
11	12	13	14	15	16	17
18	19	20	21	22	23	24
25	26	27	28	29	30	31

NOVEMBER • 2009

S	M	T	W	T	F	S
1	2	3	4	5	6	7
8	9	10	11	12	13	14
15	16	17	18	19	20	21
22	23	24	25	26	27	28
29	30					

Nevada Day

Friday 30

Today is a good day
to plant aboveground
crops.

Halloween

Saturday 31

*Q: What kind of dog
would a vampire own?*
A: A bloodhound.

Daylight Saving Time
ends at 2:00 A.M.

Sunday 1

Bearded frost,
forerunner of snow.

REMINDERS

....

....

....

....

....

Complement this calendar with daily weather and Almanac wit and wisdom at Almanac.com.

NOVEMBER with *The Old Farmer's Almanac*

MONTHLY REMINDERS

_____

_____

_____

_____

_____

_____

_____

_____

_____

_____

_____

_____

_____

_____

_____

_____

_____

_____

_____

_____

_____

_____

_____

_____

_____

_____

ASK THE ALMANAC

What can you do if your roast turkey is dry?

Slice the cooked turkey and arrange it on an ovenproof platter. Pour chicken broth over the meat and let it stand for 10 minutes in a 250°F oven to soak up the juices.

What's Your Sign?

SCORPIO

OCTOBER 23–NOVEMBER 22

Symbol: ♏ *The Scorpion*
Ruling planet: *Pluto*
Element: *Water*
Quality: *Willpower*
Ability: *To focus on goals*
Traits: *Shrewd, intuitive, passionate*

To Your Health

Looking forward to that big Thanksgiving dinner?
Here are a few ways to avoid heartburn:

🐚 Wear loose clothing. Loosen your belt, to prevent pressure on your stomach.

🐚 Do not overeat—fill your plate only once, with a reasonable amount of food. Smaller meals throughout the day are better for you.

🐚 Avoid alcohol, caffeine, carbonated drinks, chocolate, citrus, fatty or fried foods, mint, tomatoes, and spicy foods.

🐚 Eat slowly and chew thoroughly.

🐚 Avoid bending over just after the meal.

🐚 Take a walk or undertake some other light exercise an hour or two after eating to help digest your food.

🐚 Wait at least 3 hours before lying down. Before you fall asleep, elevate your head with an extra pillow.

AGE-OLD ADVICE

For heartburn, take a teaspoonful of carbonate of soda dissolved in sweetened water. Magnesia or prepared chalk is also good.

–Mrs. E. A. Howland, The American Economical Housekeeper and Family Receipt Book, *1852*

Full Beaver Moon

This month's full Moon got its name from the Algonquins, who set beaver traps at this time in order to ensure a supply of warm winter furs before the swamps froze. This Moon is also known as the Frost Moon.

🐚

On the first of November, if the weather hold clear,
An end of wheat sowing do make for the year.

Don't you think we ought to meet and talk over farm matters a little oftener? We should pick up an idea here and there that would be of use to us.

–The Old Farmer's Almanac, *November 1884*

November

2 *Monday*

Full Beaver Moon

A good life keeps off wrinkles.

3 *Tuesday*

Election Day

No popularity lives long in a democracy.

–John Quincy Adams, 6th U.S. president (1767–1848)

4 *Wednesday*

Will Rogers Day (Okla.)

In 1941, an oil well nicknamed *Petunia #1* was drilled in a flowerbed next to the Oklahoma state capitol.

5 *Thursday*

If a hen cackles inside a newlyweds' home as they are first entering, they will have a happy life together.

NOVEMBER • 2009

S	M	T	W	T	F	S
1	2	3	4	5	6	7
8	9	10	11	12	13	14
15	16	17	18	19	20	21
22	23	24	25	26	27	28
29	30					

DECEMBER • 2009

S	M	T	W	T	F	S
		1	2	3	4	5
6	7	8	9	10	11	12
13	14	15	16	17	18	19
20	21	22	23	24	25	26
27	28	29	30	31		

Friday **6**

Seasoned hardwood burns more slowly, releases more heat, and produces less creosote than softwood.

Saturday **7**

A dream of yarn indicates great possibilities to come.

Sunday **8**

You can't step twice into the same river.
–Heracleitus, Greek philosopher
(c. 540–c. 480 B.C.)

REMINDERS

....

....

....

....

....

....

November

9 *Monday*

Last Quarter

No camel route is long, with good company.
—Turkish proverb

10 *Tuesday*

Today is a good day to harvest root crops.

11 *Wednesday*

Veterans Day
Remembrance Day
(Canada)

Ice in November brings
mud in December.

12 *Thursday*

*Courage comprises
all things: A man with
courage has every
blessing.*
—Titus Maccius Plautus, Roman
dramatist (c. 254–184 B.C.)

NOVEMBER • 2009   DECEMBER • 2009

S M T W T F S   S M T W T F S
1 2 3 4 5 6 7   1 2 3 4 5
8 9 10 11 12 13 14   6 7 8 9 10 11 12
15 16 17 18 19 20 21 13 14 15 16 17 18 19
22 23 24 25 26 27 28 20 21 22 23 24 25 26
29 30   27 28 29 30 31

Friday 13

Use small bundles
of dried, woody-
stemmed herbs, such
as rosemary or bay, to
scent your fires.

Saturday 14

The flamingo has
the longest tongue of
all birds.

Sunday 15

Apply protective
mulch on the
perennial garden
after the ground has
frozen an inch or two.

REMINDERS

....
....
....
....
....
....

Complement this calendar with daily weather and Almanac wit and wisdom at Almanac.com.

NOVEMBER

16 *Monday*

New Moon

*Tailors and writers
must mind the fashion.*
—English proverb

17 *Tuesday*

On this day in 1878,
social reformer Grace
Abbott was born.

18 *Wednesday*

*Character is doing
what's right when
nobody's looking.*
—J. C. Watts Jr., America
politician (b. 1957

19 *Thursday*

Discovery Day
(Puerto Rico)

The national anima
of Puerto Rico is th
coqui tree frog.

NOVEMBER • 2009

S M T W T F S
1 2 3 4 5 6 7
8 9 10 11 12 13 14
15 16 17 18 19 20 21
22 23 24 25 26 27 28
29 30

DECEMBER • 2009

S M T W T F S
1 2 3 4 5
6 7 8 9 10 11 12
13 14 15 16 17 18 19
20 21 22 23 24 25 26
27 28 29 30 31

Today is a good day
to begin logging.

Friday 20

Sedum comes from a
Latin word meaning
"to sit," because of how
some low-growing
species grow on rocks,
walls, and walkways.

Saturday 21

To prevent a fruit
pie from becoming
soggy on the bottom,
brush the crust with
beaten egg white
before filling and
baking.

Sunday 22

REMINDERS

....
....
....
....
....
....

NOVEMBER

23 Monday

Every novel should have a beginning, a muddle, and an end.
–Peter De Vries, American editor (1910–93)

24 Tuesday

First Quarter

Think of the going out before you enter.
–Arabian proverb

25 Wednesday

Cranberries are thought to help prevent urinary tract infections, ulcers, and gum disease.

26 Thursday

Thanksgiving Day

Count each snowflake as a blessing, just like turkey and walnut dressing.
–The Old Farmer's Almanac, 195

NOVEMBER • 2009

S	M	T	W	T	F	S
1	2	3	4	5	6	7
8	9	10	11	12	13	14
15	16	17	18	19	20	21
22	23	24	25	26	27	28
29	30					

DECEMBER • 2009

S	M	T	W	T	F	S
		1	2	3	4	5
6	7	8	9	10	11	12
13	14	15	16	17	18	19
20	21	22	23	24	25	26
27	28	29	30	31		

Acadian Day (La.)

Friday 27

A hearing-impaired person may be able to understand you better if you lower the pitch of your voice.

Dream of a cow and you will receive favorable news.

Saturday 28

Sunday 29

The tolerance of differences is the measure of civilization.

–Vincent Massey, 18th governor-general of Canada (1887–1967)

REMINDERS

....
....
....
....
....

Complement this calendar with daily weather and Almanac wit and wisdom at Almanac.com.

30 *Monday*

On this day in 1954, a meteorite hit a woman in her home in Sylacauga, Alabama.

1 *Tuesday*

When the mouse laughs at the cat, there is a hole nearby.

–Nigerian proverb

2 *Wednesday*

Full Cold Moon

For best results, tap your barometer befor taking a reading.

3 *Thursday*

If the nose of Cleopatra had been shorter, the whole fac of the Earth would have been changed.

–Blaise Pascal, French scien
(1623–

NOVEMBER • 2009

S M T W T F S
1 2 3 4 5 6 7
8 9 10 11 12 13 14
15 16 17 18 19 20 21
22 23 24 25 26 27 28
29 30

DECEMBER • 2009

S M T W T F S
1 2 3 4 5
6 7 8 9 10 11 12
13 14 15 16 17 18 19
20 21 22 23 24 25 26
27 28 29 30 31

Cyclamen comes from the Greek word for "circle," because of the rounded tubers.

Friday

4

Most cookie dough freezes well for up to a month. Thaw overnight in the refrigerator.

Saturday

5

Cut a snowball in half; a wet center means rain.

Sunday

6

REMINDERS

DECEMBER with *The Old Farmer's Almanac*

MONTHLY REMINDERS

ASK THE ALMANAC

Who was St. Nicholas?

St. Nicholas likely was a 4th-century bishop of Myra in what is now Turkey. He is credited with saving three sisters from lives of ill repute by throwing bags of gold into their house to provide for their dowries. St. Nicholas's life eventually merged with folklore, and the legend of Santa Claus was born.

What's Your Sign?

SAGITTARIUS

NOVEMBER 23–DECEMBER 21

Symbol: ♐ *The Archer*
Ruling planet: *Jupiter*
Element: *Fire*
Quality: *Philosophical*
Ability: *To see the bigger picture*
Traits: *Extroverted, athletic, personable*

To Your Health

*you're flying this holiday season, here are a few tips to
keep you comfortable during your trip:*

› Get plenty of rest before you leave.

› Stay hydrated. Drink lots of water before and during
trip, and avoid alcohol and caffeine.

› If you are prone to motion sickness, ask your doctor
out medications, try a motion sickness wristband, or
some ginger before the flight. While in the air, avoid
ding, focus on an object far away, and sip ginger ale.
just the vent so that you get plenty of cool air.

› Exercise as much as possible during the flight to
intain good circulation. Walk at least once per hour,
ate your ankles, etc. Wear loose clothing. Don't cross
ur legs.

› Swallow often, yawn, or chew gum to minimize ear-
es due to changes in cabin pressure. Consider using
cial earplugs available for air travel.

› To help avoid jet lag, get used to the new time by
mediately falling in with the local schedule for meals
d sleep.

AGE-OLD ADVICE

*Good company in a journey makes the way
seem shorter.*

–Izaak Walton, English writer (1593–1683)

Full Cold Moon

DECEMBER 31

Full Long Nights Moon

*This month's Cold Moon got its
name for the time when winter
cold fastens its grip. The Long
Nights Moon was named for its
proximity to the winter solstice,
when the nights become extend-
ed. The second full Moon in a
month is also called a blue Moon.*

*If New Year's Eve night wind
blow south,
It betokeneth warmth and growth.*

man who wants to
get on in anything in
this world must give his mind to
it.

–The Old Farmer's Almanac, *December 1884*

December

7 *Monday*

To cure a cold, kiss a mu

8 *Tuesday*

Last Quarter

On this day in 154
Mary Stuart, Quee
of Scots, was born

9 *Wednesday*

*Life is a pure flame
and we live by an
invisible Sun within*

—Sir Thomas Bro
English writer (1605–

10 *Thursday*

*Q: What did one
arithmetic book say
the other arithmeti
book?*
A: "Boy, do I have
problems!"

DECEMBER • 2009   JANUARY • 2010

S M T W T F S   S M T W T F S
      1 2 3 4 5   1 2
 6 7 8 9 10 11 12   3 4 5 6 7 8 9
13 14 15 16 17 18 19   10 11 12 13 14 15 16
20 21 22 23 24 25 26   17 18 19 20 21 22 23
27 28 29 30 31   24 25 26 27 28 29 30
                       31

Friday **11**

The rare signature
of Georgia's Button
Gwinnett is one of
the most valuable
autographs of signers
of the Declaration of
Independence.

Saturday **12**

First day of Chanukah

*Where there is great
love, there are always
miracles.*
–Willa Cather, American writer
(1873–1947)

Sunday **13**

If a window shade
returns to the top too
fast, remove the
shade, unroll it a few
times, and replace it
in its hangers.

EMINDERS

....
....
....
....
....
....

December

14 Monday

Today is a good day to end old projects.

15 Tuesday

Bill of Rights Day

The Bill of Rights wa enshrined at the National Archives or this day in 1952.

16 Wednesday

New Moon

To help prevent a bathtub ring, add a few drops of baby oi to your bathwater.

17 Thursday

Wright Brothers Day

Minds are like parachutes—they on function when open

–Sir Thomas Dewar, Eng businessman (1864–19

DECEMBER • 2009

S	M	T	W	T	F	S
		1	2	3	4	5
6	7	8	9	10	11	12
13	14	15	16	17	18	19
20	21	22	23	24	25	26
27	28	29	30	31		

JANUARY • 2010

S	M	T	W	T	F	S
					1	2
3	4	5	6	7	8	9
10	11	12	13	14	15	16
17	18	19	20	21	22	23
24	25	26	27	28	29	30
31						

Friday 18

Islamic New Year

If you can not take things by the head, take them by the tail.

—Arabic proverb

Saturday 19

Fragrant herbs tucked under rugs will scent your rooms for the holidays.

Sunday 20

Use a hair dryer to thaw a frozen pipe—but be prepared to shut off the water to the area if you discover that the pipe has cracked.

REMINDERS

December

21 Monday

Winter Solstice

Jupiter has the shortest day in our solar system—approximately 9 hours 56 minutes long!

22 Tuesday

Today is a good day to cut hair to encourage growth.

23 Wednesday

Cold as the Dickens!
–The Old Farmer's Almanac, *1996*

24 Thursday

First Quarter

In Poland, a meatless dinner traditionally is served on Christmas Eve after the first star appears.

DECEMBER • 2009							JANUARY • 2010						
S	M	T	W	T	F	S	S	M	T	W	T	F	S
		1	2	3	4	5						1	2
6	7	8	9	10	11	12	3	4	5	6	7	8	9
13	14	15	16	17	18	19	10	11	12	13	14	15	16
20	21	22	23	24	25	26	17	18	19	20	21	22	23
27	28	29	30	31			24	25	26	27	28	29	30
							31						

Friday 25

Christmas Day

If the sun shines through the apple tree on Christmas Day, there will be an abundant crop next year.

Saturday 26

Boxing Day (Canada)
First day of Kwanzaa

We can not direct the wind, but we can adjust the sails.

—Bertha Calloway,
founder of the Great Plains
Black History Museum

Sunday 27

Place suet in a mesh bag and hang it from a nearby tree to treat birds to a winter feast.

REMINDERS

December

28 *Monday*

The heart has its summer and its winter.

29 *Tuesday*

Drink peppermint tea to help relieve congestion from colds, calm an upset stomach, or aid digestion.

30 *Wednesday*

A group of turtles is called a dole.

31 *Thursday*

Full Long Nights Moon

I never think of the future. It comes soon enough.
—Albert Einstein, American physicist (1879–1955)

Birthdays and Anniversaries

Name	Birthday	Anniversary

2010 Advance Planner

bold = *U.S. Federal and/or Canadian National holidays*

JANUARY • 2010

S	M	T	W	T	F	S
					1	2
3	4	5	6	7	8	9
10	11	12	13	14	15	16
17	**18**	19	20	21	22	23
24	25	26	27	28	29	30
31						

1 New Year's Day ; 18 Martin Luther King Jr.'s Birthday (observed)

FEBRUARY • 2010

S	M	T	W	T	F	S
	1	2	3	4	5	6
7	8	9	10	11	12	13
14	**15**	16	17	18	19	20
21	22	23	24	25	26	27
28						

15 George Washington's Birthday (observed)

MARCH • 2010

S	M	T	W	T	F	S
	1	2	3	4	5	6
7	8	9	10	11	12	13
14	15	16	17	18	19	20
21	22	23	24	25	26	27
28	29	30	31			

APRIL • 2010

S	M	T	W	T	F	S
				1	**2**	3
4	**5**	6	7	8	9	10
11	12	13	14	15	16	17
18	19	20	21	22	23	24
25	26	27	28	29	30	

2 Good Friday; 5 Easter Monday

MAY • 2010

S	M	T	W	T	F	S
						1
2	3	4	5	6	7	8
9	10	11	12	13	14	15
16	17	18	19	20	21	22
23	**24**	25	26	27	28	29
30	**31**					

24 Victoria Day (Canada); 31 Memorial Day (observed)

JUNE • 2010

S	M	T	W	T	F	S
		1	2	3	4	5
6	7	8	9	10	11	12
13	14	15	16	17	18	19
20	21	22	23	24	25	26
27	28	29	30			

1 Canada Day; 4 Independence Day

6 Labor Day

11 Columbus Day (observed); Thanksgiving Day (Canada)

11 Veterans Day; Remembrance Day (Canada); 25 Thanksgiving Day

25 Christmas Day; 26 Boxing Day (Canada)

JULY • 2010

S	M	T	W	T	F	S
				1	2	3
4	5	6	7	8	9	10
11	12	13	14	15	16	17
18	19	20	21	22	23	24
25	26	27	28	29	30	31

AUGUST • 2010

S	M	T	W	T	F	S
1	2	3	4	5	6	7
8	9	10	11	12	13	14
15	16	17	18	19	20	21
22	23	24	25	26	27	28
29	30	31				

SEPTEMBER • 2010

S	M	T	W	T	F	S
			1	2	3	4
5	**6**	7	8	9	10	11
12	13	14	15	16	17	18
19	20	21	22	23	24	25
26	27	28	29	30		

OCTOBER • 2010

S	M	T	W	T	F	S
					1	2
3	4	5	6	7	8	9
10	**11**	12	13	14	15	16
17	18	19	20	21	22	23
24	25	26	27	28	29	30
31						

NOVEMBER • 2010

S	M	T	W	T	F	S
	1	2	3	4	5	6
7	8	9	10	**11**	12	13
14	15	16	17	18	19	20
21	22	23	24	**25**	26	27
28	29	30				

DECEMBER • 2010

S	M	T	W	T	F	S
			1	2	3	4
5	6	7	8	9	10	11
12	13	14	15	16	17	18
19	20	21	22	23	24	**25**
26	27	28	29	30	31	

Complement this calendar with daily weather and Almanac wit and wisdom at Almanac.com.

2011 Advance Planner

bold = *U.S. Federal and/or Canadian National holidays*

JANUARY • 2011

S	M	T	W	T	F	S
						1
2	3	4	5	6	7	8
9	10	11	12	13	14	15
16	**17**	18	19	20	21	22
23	24	25	26	27	28	29
30	31					

FEBRUARY • 2011

S	M	T	W	T	F	S
		1	2	3	4	5
6	7	8	9	10	11	12
13	14	15	16	17	18	19
20	**21**	22	23	24	25	26
27	28					

MARCH • 2011

S	M	T	W	T	F	S
		1	2	3	4	5
6	7	8	9	10	11	12
13	14	15	16	17	18	19
20	21	22	23	24	25	26
27	28	29	30	31		

APRIL • 2011

S	M	T	W	T	F	S
					1	2
3	4	5	6	7	8	9
10	11	12	13	14	15	16
17	18	19	20	21	**22**	23
24	**25**	26	27	28	29	30

MAY • 2011

S	M	T	W	T	F	S
1	2	3	4	5	6	7
8	9	10	11	12	13	14
15	16	17	18	19	20	21
22	**23**	24	25	26	27	28
29	**30**	31				

JUNE • 2011

S	M	T	W	T	F	S
			1	2	3	4
5	6	7	8	9	10	11
12	13	14	15	16	17	18
19	20	21	22	23	24	25
26	27	28	29	30		

JULY • 2011

S	M	T	W	T	F	S
					1	2
3	**4**	5	6	7	8	9
10	11	12	13	14	15	16
17	18	19	20	21	22	23
24	25	26	27	28	29	30
31						

AUGUST • 2011

S	M	T	W	T	F	S
	1	2	3	4	5	6
7	8	9	10	11	12	13
14	15	16	17	18	19	20
21	22	23	24	25	26	27
28	29	30	31			

SEPTEMBER • 2011

S	M	T	W	T	F	S
				1	2	3
4	**5**	6	7	8	9	10
11	12	13	14	15	16	17
18	19	20	21	22	23	24
25	26	27	28	29	30	

OCTOBER • 2011

S	M	T	W	T	F	S
						1
2	3	4	5	6	7	8
9	**10**	11	12	13	14	15
16	17	18	19	20	21	22
23	24	25	26	27	28	29
30	31					

NOVEMBER • 2011

S	M	T	W	T	F	S
		1	2	3	4	5
6	7	8	9	10	11	12
13	14	15	16	17	18	19
20	21	22	23	**24**	25	26
27	28	29	30			

DECEMBER • 2011

S	M	T	W	T	F	S
				1	2	3
4	5	6	7	8	9	10
11	12	13	14	15	16	17
18	19	20	21	22	23	24
25	**26**	27	28	29	30	31

Addresses and Phone Numbers

Name _____ Home _____
Address _____ Work _____
_____ Cell _____
E-mail _____ Fax _____
Web site _____

Name _____ Home _____
Address _____ Work _____
_____ Cell _____
E-mail _____ Fax _____
Web site _____

Name _____ Home _____
Address _____ Work _____
_____ Cell _____
E-mail _____ Fax _____
Web site _____

Name _____ Home _____
Address _____ Work _____
_____ Cell _____
E-mail _____ Fax _____
Web site _____

Name _____ Home _____
Address _____ Work _____
_____ Cell _____
E-mail _____ Fax _____
Web site _____

Name _____ Home _____
Address _____ Work _____
_____ Cell _____
E-mail _____ Fax _____
Web site _____

Complement this calendar with daily weather and Almanac wit and wisdom at Almanac.com.

Emergency Numbers

In case of emergency, notify:

Name _____ Relationship _____

Address _____

_____

Phone _____ E-mail _____

Police Department _____

Fire Department _____

Ambulance _____

Hospital _____

Poison Control _____

Physician _____

Dentist _____

Veterinarian _____

Pharmacy _____

Clergy _____

Electric Company _____

Electrician _____

Plumber _____

Auto Mechanic _____

Baby-sitter _____

School(s) _____

Insurance:

   Auto _____

   Health _____

   Dental _____

   Homeowner's _____

Other _____

_____

_____

_____

_____

_____

_____